THE SPIRIT OF WEST POINT
Celebrating 200 Years

Jon C. Malinowski & Eugene J. Palka

Original Illustrations by Robert A. Getz

BLACK·DOME
Black Dome Press Corp.
1011 Route 296 Hensonville, New York 12439
Tel: (518) 734-6357 Fax: (518) 734-5802
www.blackdomepress.com

Published by

BLACK DOME PRESS CORP.
1011 Route 296
Hensonville, New York 12439
Tel: (518) 734-6357
Fax: (518) 734-5802
www.blackdomepress.com

ISBN 1-883789-30-3

Library of Congress Cataloging-in-Publication Data:

Malinowski, Jon C.
    The spirit of West Point : celebrating 200 years / by Jon C. Malinowski & Eugene J.
Palka ; original illustrations by Robert A. Getz.
       p. cm.
    Includes bibliographical references.
    ISBN 1-883789-30-3 (trade paper)
     1. United States Military Academy—History—Pictorial works. I. Palka, Eugene Joseph.
II. Title.

U410.L3 M35 2001
355'.0071'173—dc21

                                                            2001043675

Cover: The bicentennial class of 2002 marches as part of the Oath Review on Reception Day 1998.
Photo courtesy of the Creative Imaging Branch, Directorate of Information Management, USMA.
Inset: West Point and the Hudson Highlands, 2001.
Photo by John Pellino, Creative Imaging Branch, DOIM, USMA.

Back cover: Cadets on R-Day courtesy of the Creative Imaging Branch, DOIM, USMA.
Cadets on Parade Field, Photo by John Pellino Creative Imaging Branch, DOIM, USMA.

Design by Carol Clement, Artemisia, Inc.
Printed in the USA

THE SPIRIT OF WEST POINT
Celebrating 200 Years

Contents

Preface

During the Revolutionary War from 1775 to 1783, the lower Hudson River Valley witnessed a significant amount of military activity as the Continental and British Armies struggled to gain control of the Hudson River. American and British commanders alike recognized the strategic importance of the Hudson River as a major thoroughfare into the interior of the colonies and as a vital link between New England and the Middle-Atlantic. A concerted effort was made by the Continental Army to construct and fortify positions along the lower Hudson in order to protect crossing sites, ensure the continued flow of logistics and commerce, and prevent the British from using the river as a major thoroughfare to transport troops and supplies. Benedict Arnold's attempted sale to the British of plans detailing the configuration of fortifications at West Point is a legendary chapter in American history.

Among the remnants of the Revolutionary War landscape, West Point and its environs are perhaps the most distinctive and most celebrated. The United States flag has been flown at West Point since 1778, and the post has housed the United States Military Academy since 1802. It is on the post-Revolution importance of West Point as the home of the Military Academy that this book focuses. The details of the Great Chain, George Washington's strategic vision, and Arnold's treason are well documented elsewhere.

On the eve of its bicentennial celebration, West Point is still remembered as America's "Rock of Gibraltar" in some respects. Perhaps more importantly, however, the United States Military Academy has continued to maintain a reputation as one of the premier leadership institutions in the world. The academy and its historic surroundings attract more than 2.5 million visitors each year. This book will serve to enhance understanding of the historical significance of West Point, the Academy's evolution over the past two hundred years, and the continual role that the celebrated leader-producing institution plays today.

Battle Monument

The "Spirit" of West Point

Mere space becomes a place once people impart meaning to it. A place is an areal extent, locale or setting that has boundaries, location and significance, at least in the mind of the beholder. We can think of places in either the general or specific sense. A desert or forest is an example of the former, while Pittsburgh, Pennsylvania, or a certain room in one's house exemplifies the latter. We rely on places to provide the framework for our mental maps. Most places even evoke some type of emotional response. The "spirit of a place" helps one to distinguish that place from all others, providing an identity that may endure for generations.

The "spirit" of a place stems from both natural and cultural phenomena over time. Natural phenomena provide the context for human existence and include such attributes as the local vegetation, relief, climate, drainage patterns, and fauna. Obvious cultural aspects of a place include the built environment, human activities, and the imprint created by collective efforts to carve a niche out of the specific locale. Less obvious are superstitions, myths, legends, feelings of anxiety or affection, or the expectations that people attach to a specific place.

Since people continually interact with each other, as well as with the natural environment, all places are always in the process of "becoming," despite the enduring reputations that some may attain. This notion is especially important to places like West Point, where millions of visitors arrive each year to experience this historical institution and setting. Moreover, new cadets enter the academy each year, as do new members of the staff and faculty. Regardless of their capacity, each person brings various preconceived notions about the place and experiences a wide range of emotions during the course of their visit or stay. These same people, either consciously or not, contribute to the spirit of the place during their tenure or even after they depart.

The spirit of a place, then, evolves over time and refers to aspects of its reputation, personality, and characteristics that contribute to an enduring identity. People can experience the spirit of a place whenever they interact with that particular place, either mentally or physically. One need not be on the Plain at West Point to appreciate the spirit of the place. Simple recollections, a published book or article, or the mere mention of the U.S. Military Academy at West Point during the course of a discussion among people halfway around the world can conjure up mental images and emotional sensations that help to distinguish this place from any other.

What are the attributes of West Point that contribute to the spirit of the place? Common experiences, visual cues, and stories promote consensus images and feelings about West Point. Cadets, faculty or staff members, and visitors routinely collaborate about various aspects of the place. Feelings of pride, professionalism, or even frustration can help the consensus images or impressions to endure for generations. This widely acclaimed institution, historic site, and artistic landscape has always attracted world famous visitors. How is it that this special place continues to bring out the best in people? Why do people invariably depart with a deep sense of pride, respect, and fulfillment?

This book examines a range of human and natural phenomena that have contributed to the spirit of West Point during the course of its 200 years of existence. We have selected several categories that have significance to anyone who has ever visited, attended, or worked at West Point. It is our hope that by examining some of the enduring themes within each of our selected areas, readers will better understand the spirit of West Point. Additionally, we hope to assist readers in developing a personal and enduring "sense of place" regarding this special institution and hallowed ground regardless of their affiliation or familiarity.

CHAPTER ONE

Our Rockbound Highland Home

Territorial Expansion

The military reservation at West Point has continually evolved since its use during the American Revolution. Most people are only familiar with the main post or built-up area, yet the reservation expands outward from the Plain for more than 16,000 acres. Our focus will be on the "experienced landscape," that is, the portion of West Point that falls within the activity space of cadets, faculty, staff, and visitors. The historical significance of the main post area was formally recognized in 1960, when it was dedicated as a National Historic Landmark.

Despite numerous changes to the size and organization of the West Point reservation and to the main post area over the past 200 years, one of the constant reference points has been the view from Trophy Point looking north up the Hudson River Valley towards Newburgh.

1780

This mid-nineteenth-century engraving depicts West Point near the end of the Revolution. West Point was a vital link in the Continental strategy to prevent the British from controlling the River. British control would have meant the colonies would be cut in two, making a unified Continental effort much more difficult.

Chosen for its physical geography, West Point became a formidable defensive position. The "s"-shaped curve in the Hudson River required sailing ships to slow down to navigate the turns. Gun positions on Constitution Island were supported and protected by Fort Clinton on the plain of West Point and redoubts on the surrounding hills. A large chain was floated from West Point to Constitution Island to further discourage British ships from attempting to pass the position. It was never tested.

Fort Clinton (previously Fort Arnold before his treason) dominates the foreground overlooking the Hudson. Smaller batteries can be seen on the slopes below. Just to the left of the fort is Long Barracks, built during the Revolution and a part of the landscape until destroyed by fire in 1826. Further to the left a few other buildings can be seen. These functioned as quarters and supply houses. At the top left is Fort Putnam, overlooking and protecting the Plain below. Notice the lack of tree cover. Wood was used as material for fortifications and other buildings, fuel for cooking, and as an industrial resource to create charcoal for iron furnaces. Land was also cleared, of course, for agricultural uses.

1830s

Fifty years produced a lot of changes in the built landscape. The details of this time are discussed on the next two pages. What is clear is the addition of many institutional buildings. The largest two, in the middle, are North and South Barracks. The Academy Building and Mess Hall are to their right, and further along are officers' quarters. Dating this image is difficult, but the small building to the left of the large barracks could be the Old Cadet Chapel, built in 1836. The absence of the library (built in 1841) to the left suggests this image is from the 1830s at the latest. If that is not the Chapel to the left of the barracks, the engraving could be earlier. North Barracks was constructed in 1817. In any case, notice the almost complete lack of Fort Clinton ruins in the foreground.

1830

This map is from about 1830 and provides a good overview of the Academy at that time. As today, most of the administrative buildings are located on the southern side of the Plain. The Superintendent's House (A), built in 1820 on the site of a two-story wooden building that served as the Superintendent's quarters and as classroom space, and the Commandant's House, dated by some to

1819, are the only remaining buildings from this time. The Cadet Mess (B) was built in 1815 and torn down in 1853 when the old Grant Hall went into service as the mess. It was a two-story, stone and stucco facility. The Academy Building (C and pictured on the next page) held classrooms, offices, and laboratory facilities. A two-story stone building, it was built in 1815 and was used until a

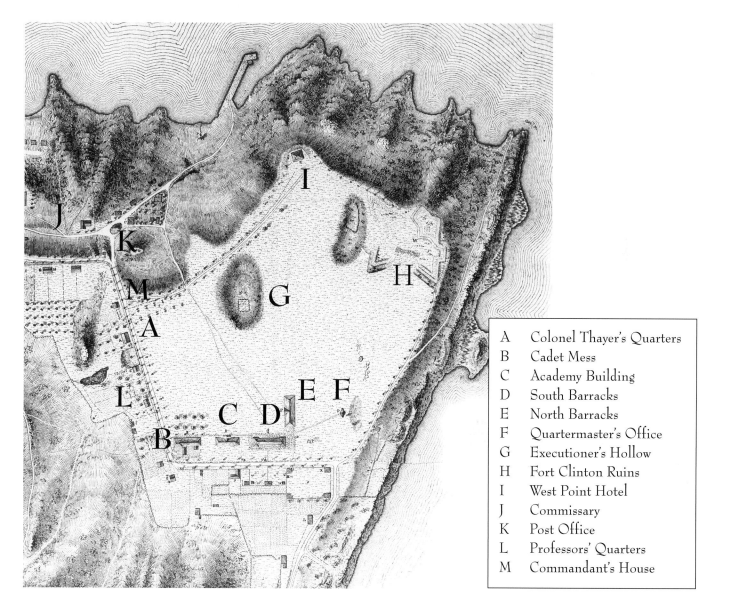

A	Colonel Thayer's Quarters
B	Cadet Mess
C	Academy Building
D	South Barracks
E	North Barracks
F	Quartermaster's Office
G	Executioner's Hollow
H	Fort Clinton Ruins
I	West Point Hotel
J	Commissary
K	Post Office
L	Professors' Quarters
M	Commandant's House

fire destroyed it, and most of the Academy's records, in 1838. South Barracks (D and pictured above) was a three-story, stone and stucco structure built in 1815, and North Barracks, the Academy's first four-storied building, was built in 1817. The barracks replaced the wooden Revolutionary-era Long Barracks, located on Trophy Point until destroyed by fire in 1826.

Executioner's Hollow (G) supposedly refers to a location where prisoners were put to death during the Revolution. It has since been filled in completely. The Fort Clinton ruins persisted for much of the 19th century before most were leveled or worn down. Other support buildings and housing were scattered to the north and south of the main campus.

1867

By the end of the Civil War, the Academy had expanded its facilities. The superintendent's quarters remained with other faculty homes along the western edge of the Plain while academic and administrative buildings dominated the southern side. This map shows many of the new buildings that had been built during the mid-nineteenth century, many during the tenure of Superintendent Richard Delafield.

From left to right across the southern margin of the Plain, the first building (P) was the L-shaped Cadet Barracks, built between 1849 and 1851 and used until the 1960s. All that remains of these barracks is the old 1st Division in Central Area which houses Nininger Hall, site of cadet honor hearings. To the east was the Second Academy (R), built in 1838 and used until demolition in 1891.

Across the road was the old Cadet Chapel (S), a classically inspired building completed in 1836. Next to it was the old library, completed in 1841 and used until 1961 when it was torn down to allow for the present facility. Along the water were the stables (X) and a riding hall (W), both built in the mid-1850s and used until the first decade of the 20th century. At the time, the Riding Hall was the largest building of its type in the country.

To the south of the Academy (R), a new mess hall (U) was erected in 1851. This would later be known as Grant Hall. Further down the road, a hospital (V) could be found. It was built in 1834 and used until a new hospital was built in about the same location in 1884.

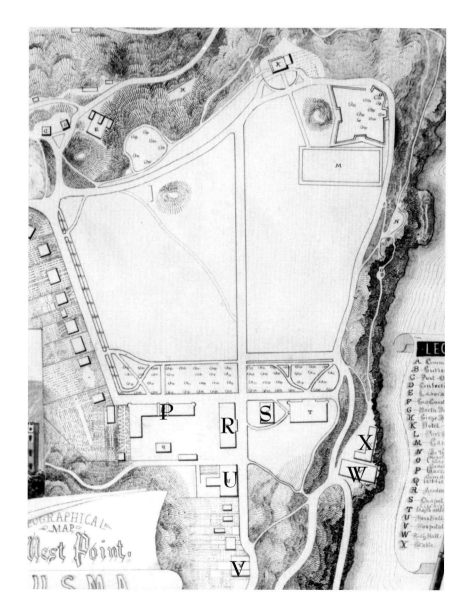

1908

The turn of the century brought tremendous change for the Academy, as depicted in this 1908 map showing many buildings during their construction.

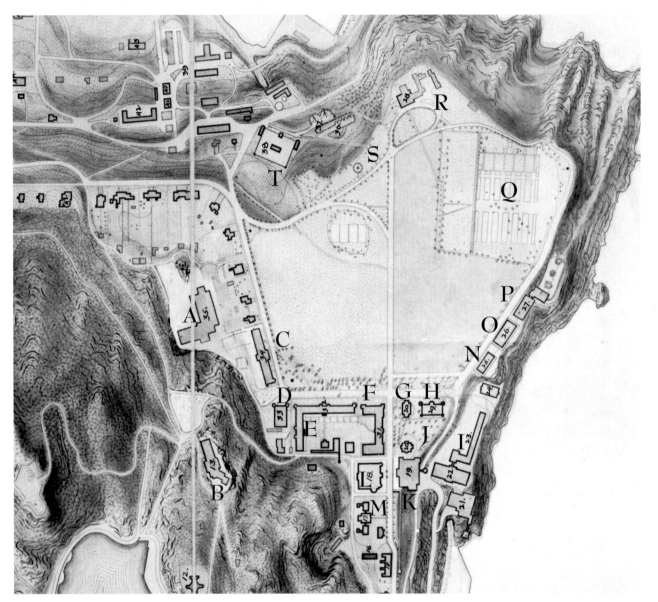

A	Gymnasium (completed 1910)	K	New Administration Building (1910) now Taylor Hall
B	Cadet Chapel (completed 1910)	L	Grant Hall (1851–1929)
C	North Barracks (completed 1909)	M	Hospital
D	Old Gym (1891–1924)	N	West Point Army Mess (1903)
E	Central Barracks	O	Cullum Hall (1896)
F	West Academic Building (1895) now Pershing Barracks	P	Bachelor Officers' Quarters (completed 1910) now Lincoln Hall
G	Old Chapel (1836, moved in 1910)	Q	Summer Camp Area
H	Library (1841–1861)	R	West Point Hotel
I	Riding Hall and Stables	S	Battle Monument (1897)
J	Old Administration Building (1871–1910)	T	Ordnance Compound

1917

This 1917 map of West Point focuses on the main post area and vicinity. Individual academy buildings and housing are easily identifiable with few changes from the previous 1908 map. The map also shows the locations of old Revolutionary redoubts, including two (Webb and Wyllis) in what is now the Lusk Reservoir housing area. Notice that the area along the Hudson below the Plain on the north is labeled as a Polo Field and Target Range, two activities no longer practiced on the main post.

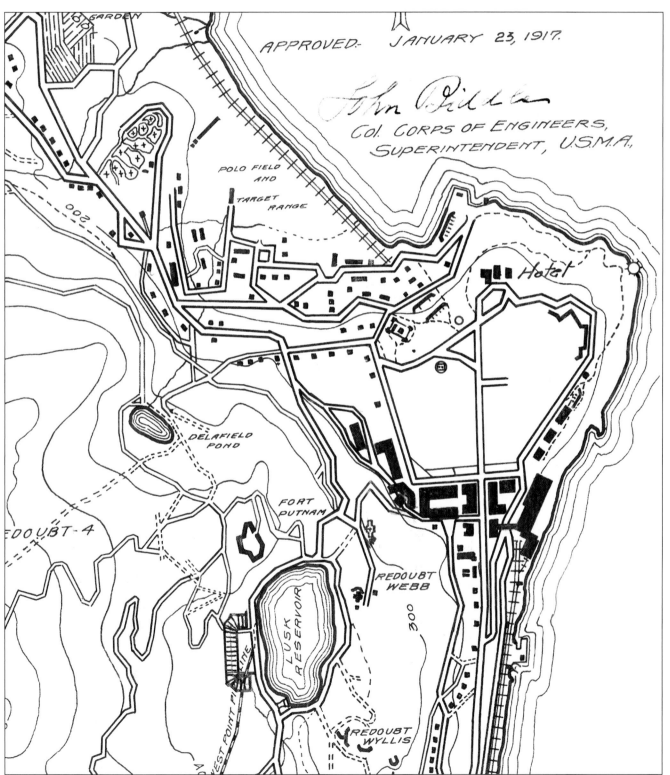

This pre-1925 photograph provides an aerial view from the east looking west towards the Cadet Chapel. Notice the twin towers of the old gymnasium below the Chapel and the old Library on the east side of the Plain. Also notice the tennis courts in front of the Library, the lack of seating at Doubleday baseball field, and the summer training camp area in the right foreground. Before the days of training at Camp Buckner, cadets spent their summers here in tents, providing a constant spectacle for visiting tourists staying at the nearby West Point Hotel. These tourists also provided social opportunities for cadets.

As opposed to the previous map, an official engineer product, the map closeups depicted on these pages represent a cadet's perspective of West Point in 1930, when the map appeared in the *Howitzer* yearbook. North is at the top.

In the closeup of the Plain, cadets can be seen marching, playing football, lacrosse, and tennis, studying (a stack of books represents the library), and pulling guard duty in the summer camp area. Cullum Hall, long a site of hops, is portrayed with dancers on top. Next door, in what is now Lincoln Hall, laundry fittingly hangs out the window of what used to be bachelor officers quarters. Horses sticking out of what is now Thayer Hall symbolize its long function as the riding hall.

Other items of interest include the general's stars by the superintendent's house, vegetable gardens behind officers houses, the location of Washington Monument at the north end of the Plain (with arm raised), the location of the West Point Hotel at Trophy Point, and the beer mug at the Firstie Club just north of the flag pole.

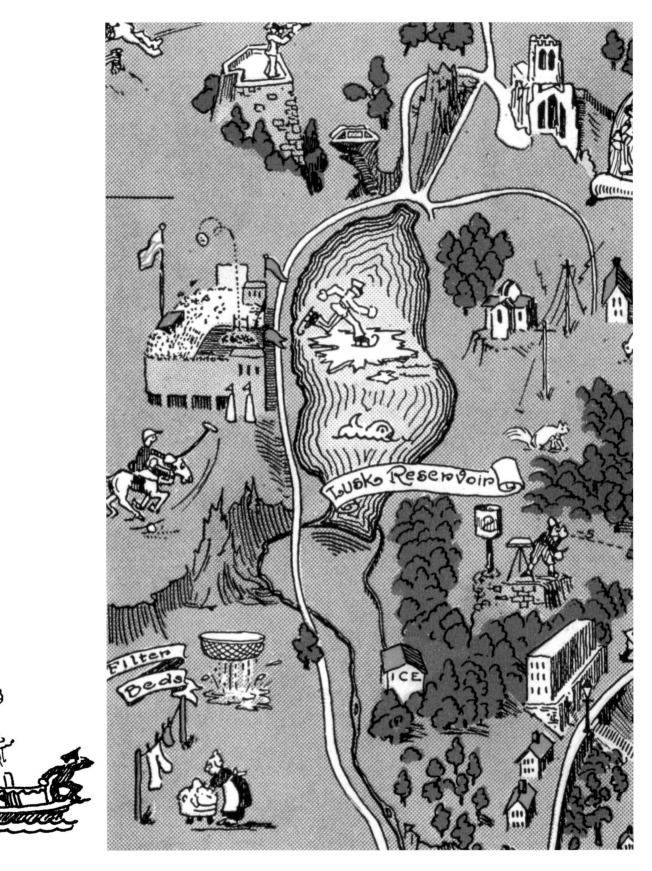

Above is a portion of the 1930 map showing the Lusk Reservoir area. Included are Michie Stadium without seats along the road side, ice skating on Lusk, the old observatory, an old icehouse, and filter beds for water treatment.

Above are details of Camp Buckner around Lake Popolopen, which began to be used during this time as part of summer training activities. With names like Camp Freezeout, Hellhole, and The Torne, cadets apparently were not thrilled with their new training grounds.

21

17 WEST POINT N.Y.

FROM THE AIR

This 1930s aerial photo provides "ground truth" for the perceptual maps on the previous two pages. The view is looking north up the Hudson River Valley, with Constitution Island in the center-right of the picture. The famous "bend" in the river is also obvious. This bend required ships to slow to make the corner, allowing for better bombardment from shore. Less speed also made it less likely that a warship would have enough force to break aquatic defenses, such as the Great Chain that stretched from West Point to Constitution Island.

This is a 1944 aerial photograph looking south across the main post area towards Highland Falls. Lusk Reservoir, Michie Stadium, and Fort Putnam are clearly visible in the background. Note that Washington Hall at the south end of the Plain has yet to be expanded, making the tree-lined Plain larger than it is today. Note also that Thayer Road extends across the Plain. Today, cars must travel around this area.

This July 1961 south-looking photograph shows in greater detail the arrangement of the Plain that many graduates will remember. Parade visitors would line the southern side of the Plain in front of the barracks to watch the cadets march. The old library (and tennis courts), the original, unexpanded Washington Hall, and the absence of any baseball stadium are obvious differences from today's landscape. Thayer Road still cuts across the Plain during this time, ending at the statue of Washington near the Battle Monument. Both monuments are partially visible near the bottom of the photo.

The aerial photograph was taken from above the Hudson River in the early 1970s, looking south. In the foreground is North Dock and the old book warehouse, long since leveled and recently paved over as a parking lot. The view of the Plain pre-dates modifications to the parade field, reviewing stand, and the road that provides the left (east) boundary of the Plain. Note, too, that Eisenhower Hall has not yet been built.

Looking out of a window of Washington Hall, this picture captures a parade during graduation week of 1999. Washington Monument, Washington Hall, and the Chapel now serve as a fitting backdrop for cadet reviews. In the past, as seen in the 1965 photo at the top of the facing page, guests sat with Washington Hall at their backs.

Looking east from Michie Stadium across Lusk Reservoir more than 60 years ago (bottom), the Lusk Housing Area boasts center-hall Colonial style homes. Today the homes are completely concealed by a stand of tall pines.

...and a butt*...

The new Lee Housing Area appears like a modern suburban subdivision in this 1944 photo.

* "Butt" is cadet slang for anything leftover, as in, "There are 36 and a butt days until Army beats the Hell out of Navy!"

CHAPTER TWO

The Corps, and the Corps, and the Corps

Cadet Life

From the time new cadets report to "the cadet with the red sash" on R-Day until the time they throw their hats into the air on graduation day, cadet life is full of challenges. Cadets and graduates alike will agree that West Point is relentless in every respect—academically, militarily, physically, and emotionally. Nevertheless, cadets have always found time to laugh at various aspects of cadet life. Cadet humor is rooted in a common experience.

Robert A. Getz

The Emblem of the Military Academy emphasizes the dual nature of cadet life. On one hand, the sword represents the profession of arms and reminds that all cadets will be officers. The helmet, however, is that of the Greek goddess Pallas Athena and stands for learning and wisdom.

Thus, the emblem remains an appropriate reminder of West Point as a military college. The emblem was introduced in the late 19th century. Versions before 1923 often have the sword and helmet reversed. The current form came into effect to better meet the rules of heraldry.

Reception Day

Regardless of whether one inprocessed nearly two centuries ago or along with the bicentennial class of 2002, memories of "R-Day" are charged with emotion and recollections of a queasy stomach for most grads.

Note the measuring stick to determine a new cadet's height. This young man happens to be an international new cadet from the Philippines.

Wearing a mixture of newly issued cadet uniforms and civilian clothes, new cadets (in the foreground) form up in Central Area in 1926. Cadets marching in the center of the picture are further along in the reception process, as evidenced by their complete uniforms. Upper class cadre members sport the "dress gray over white" uniform, long abandoned during "Beast Barracks" for the more seasonably comfortable "white over gray" uniform.

R-Day in 1970 reveals a distinct difference in acceptable hairstyles than the previous 1926 photo. New cadets sport T-shirts with plastic name tags, the classic "one size fits all" gym shorts, black socks with little or no elastic, and low quarters. As previously noted, cadre members are donned in the white over gray summer uniform. Note the tags attached to the shorts of the new cadets. Graduates will recall the memory of having the tag "checked off" as they proceed from one station to the next during the reception process.

Below right, R-Day for the class of 2002 highlights the co-ed nature of the corps and a few changes in clothing styles, but the expressions and the nature of the experience are essentially unchanged.

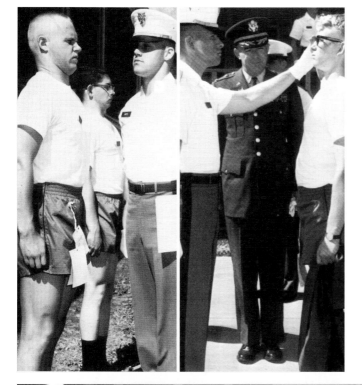

Cadet Rooms

The cadet room above dates to 1879. Some enduring practices are evident. Note the use of name tags over the beds and bookcases. Books appear to be in descending order of size on the bookshelf, and bedding is neatly displayed on the "unmade" bed to discourage sleeping during the course of the day. Bedding still consists of a combination of sheets, wool blankets, and a quilt.

The 1907 room to the left shows the cadet uniforms displayed in the closet in order of increasing formality from right to left. Laundry bags are hung from hooks on the rear wall. Later changes in bunk styles enabled the laundry bags to be hung from a bedpost at the foot of the bed.

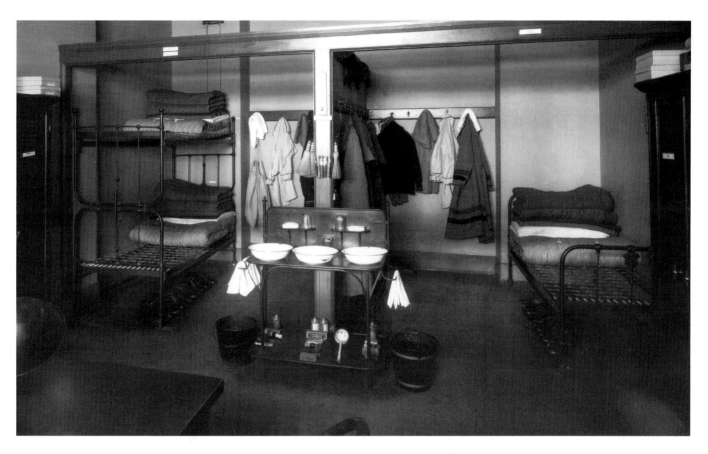

This is a 1916 view of a three-man room. Today, cadets still are housed in two or three-person rooms depending on the barracks and the size of the company. The three-man room necessitates the use of a bunk-bed.

Note the shoes prominently aligned and displayed under the bed. Hanging from the hook is the coveted "B-robe," customarily decorated with various types of insignia.

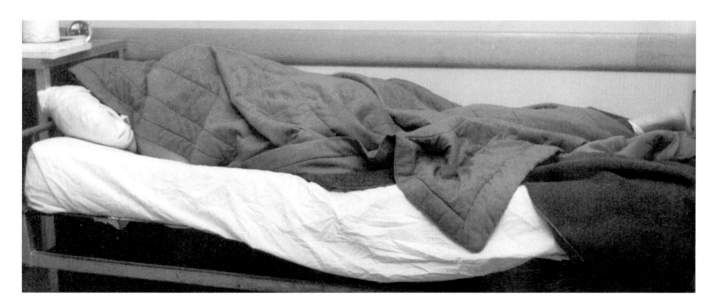

Affectionately called "green girls" (or "brown boys" by female cadets) for much of the Academy's history, most graduates and present-day cadets would agree that this simple quilt is one of West Point's few creature comforts.

This scene in 1978 has been experienced by a countless number of cadets over the years. It doesn't get any better than a cold and rainy Friday afternoon with no drill, parade, intramural, or corps squad competition.

This 1914 photograph reveals the cadet uniforms of the time. Although the field training uniforms have remained consistent with the styles of the regular Army (note the cadets in the rear left and right), the distinctive West Point uniforms have changed little. The long over-coat (middle rear), the dress gray under arms (left front), the full dress whites (middle front), and the full dress (right front) have undergone little modification. Aside from replacing the M-1 rifle with an M-14, only the gray and white hats have changed slightly. Still today, the feathered plume on the cadet "tar-bucket" (right front) is indicative of a first class cadet, while all other classes boast a "pom-pom" on their full dress hat.

Maintaining cadet uniforms is another issue. Although the post laundry and dry cleaning service is a highly efficient, top-quality operation, cadet perspectives differ on the nature of the support, as indicated by this 1930 cartoon below. Over the years plebes have been the first and last step in the process, dutifully collecting dirty laundry and dry cleaning and "sending it out," then subsequently delivering the packages and pieces upon return. Below left, an enthusiastic plebe attends to his dry cleaning duties in 1967.

Prior to the construction of the present day mess hall in Washington Hall in 1929, cadets ate their meals in Grant Hall. This February 1924 photo shows cadets at the dinner meal. It is relatively easy to distinguish the plebes at each of the tables. The ten-person table endures, as do the waiters dressed in whites, and the practice of draping the long overcoats, or any outer garment over the backs of the chairs.

Washington Hall - South End - Graduation Hop 1929

This interior view of Washington Hall has been experienced by only a few. The photo above was taken prior to the graduation hop in 1929, shortly after the mess hall's completion a few months earlier. Although the mess hall continues to be used for banquets, formal affairs, and dances, the tables of each wing are normally kept in place, while the area around the "poop deck" is used to accommodate the orchestra and dancing.

37

At West Point, it usually doesn't take much to make some people happy, as indicated by the plebes at right in this 1956 photo of a "mess hall rally."

As opposed to the display of enthusiasm, however genuine, the new cadets above do not seem to be enjoying a "full and sufficient" meal in this 1967 mess hall scene. Over the years there has been much discussion as to whether eating was a "right" or "privilege." Along the same lines, the mess hall seemed to be an ideal place for helping cadets to master self-discipline, restraint, composure, and other attributes.

TARGET—
THAT GUNNER

Cadet life also includes drill and ceremony. No piece of real estate has been used more intensively by cadets than "The Plain." Here, in 1904, cadets conduct cavalry training on a dusty and worn Plain. Battle Monument appears in the rear center, and the old West Point Hotel is visible on the right.

Adjacent to Doubleday Field is a grass field that has served multiple purposes over the years. This 1903 photo shows cadets undergoing bayonet training. Note that dress gray is the training uniform of the day. Here the cadets complete the "butt stroke" to the head series with their M-1 rifles. The newly constructed officers' mess appears in the rear center, and Cullum Hall is to the left. Cadets continue to use the same field today for intramural soccer, volleyball, and physical fitness training.

...and a butt...

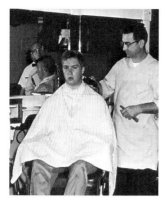

CHAPTER THREE

Take Boards!

Academics

Since the Academy's birth date in 1802, cadet life has revolved around the academic program. For more than nine months of the year, cadets are challenged by what is regarded by many as the toughest undergraduate curriculum in the world. With its broad range of required course offerings, West Point has managed its curriculum to be forward-looking and to stay abreast of the needs of the Army to prepare cadets for a lifetime of service to the country. The program provides a broad education with firm grounding in the math, science, engineering, humanities, and social science arenas and produces a noteworthy number of Rhodes, Hertz, and Truman scholars every year.

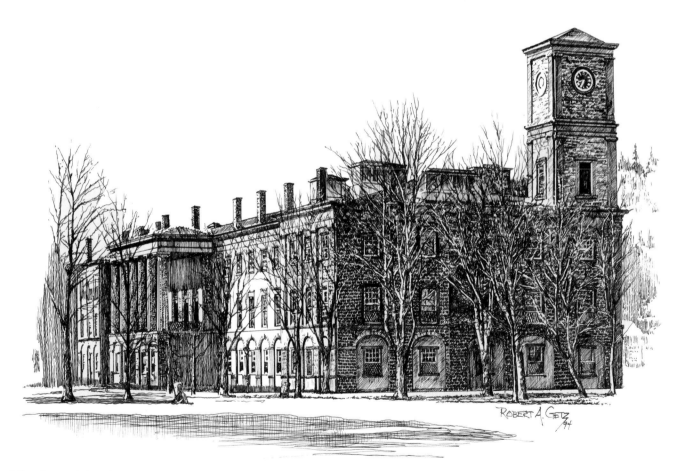

The Second Academy, 1838-1891.

Although known today as Pershing Barracks, this building was the West Academic Building from its construction in 1895 until being converted to cadet quarters in 1959.

Requiring cadets to recite in class has long been an integral aspect of the "Thayer method." Above, in 1903, a cadet explains his position to the class. Note that the class uniforms are cadet gray instead of the class shirt over gray trousers worn today.

The four photographs on these two pages are a fortuitous example of repeat photography within the academic arena. All represent the same class, an engineering fundamentals course in technical drawing. Although the course changed over the years to meet technological and military needs, the basic structure of the cadet experience seems to have changed little. The last three pictures were actually taken in the same Washington Hall drafting room!

Pictured above circa 1900 is Professor Charles Larned, Head of the Department of Drawing and a powerful member of the Academic Board for many years.

Half a century later, in 1944, cadets during the war years were taking the same course with similar t-squares, triangles, and white shirts.

There doesn't appear to be a great deal of difference between the cadet engineering fundamentals class in 1956 (above) and 1965 (below). Both photographs were taken in the same classroom in Washington Hall. By 1965, however, drafting table designs had evolved to the point where cadets could conveniently place additional books on the underside of the table to create more work space.

Computer instruction in 1963 was conducted *en masse*. Cadets listen to a lecture explaining the "state of the art" technology at that time. Today, every cadet has a high-speed personal computer on his/her desk in the barracks. Cadets continue, however, to take basic computer science as a required course.

Here, cadets receive a bit of "hands-on" training following the lecture above. Hardware at the time was large and cumbersome by today's standards.

By the early 1970s (right), advancements in computer technology enabled cadets to spend more personal learning time in computer labs and individual terminals scattered throughout the barracks area.

Cadets have always seemed to welcome instruction outside of the classroom. This is a terrain analysis class conducted at Fort Putnam, overlooking the Cadet Chapel and the Plain.

Field trips away from West Point continue to be perceived as "a good deal." Here, cadets participate in a field trip to New York City's Hayden Planetarium in February of 1952. Field trips during winter months, however, always included the requirement to wear the long overcoat, an extra 15 pounds.

It is always a challenge for cadets to convince their instructor of their personal knowledge and understanding. Impressing one's classmates, however, is even more difficult as depicted in this 1950 classroom photograph.

Wherever possible, instructors incorporate visual aids and teaching ancillaries within the classroom. Below, in a 1965 astronomy class, an instructor incorporates models to help simplify earth-sun relationships.

...and a butt...

CHAPTER FOUR

Fields of Friendly Strife

Athletics

As the late General Douglas MacArthur explained, "every cadet is an athlete." The continued emphasis on physical fitness has long been understood by an institution that is charged with ensuring that its graduates are mentally and physically fit to lead soldiers in battle. Aside from the physical fitness that is an integral part of their military training, cadets are required to take a physical fitness class every semester, and to participate in intramural sports throughout the year if they are not participating in a varsity or club sport. Talk about competitive spirit!!!! West Point's intramural (or intramurder) program was even featured in Sports Illustrated a few years ago. In addition to fostering personal conditioning and athletic development, all of the athletic programs facilitate team building, enhance cohesion and cooperation, and instill a sense of pride.

The old gymnasium stood on the present site of Washington Hall from 1891 until 1924.

Army vs. Navy, 1915 (right)

Army football in the early 1920s was played on the field adjacent to Doubleday and Clinton Fields. Note the old West Point Hotel in the background with Battle Monument to the left rear.

Opposite above right, Doc Blanchard (number 35) and Glenn Davis (number 41) are synonymous with Army's celebrated football history. The pair were Army's first two of three Heisman Trophy winners.

Opposite above left, Pete Dawkins, class of 1959, was Army's third Heisman Trophy winner (wearing number 24).

The top picture on this page shows the south end of newly constructed Michie Stadium in 1928. The stadium was named after Dennis Mahan Michie (class of 1892), who captained and coached the first Army football team in 1892. He was later killed during the Spanish-American War in 1898. Still the home of Army football, the stadium has been renovated and upgraded to hold more than 40,000 people.

Coach Earl "Red" Blaik (left) set a coaching standard that few can rival. He guided Army to six undefeated seasons and three national championships. This photo was taken on the practice field in 1951. A member of the National Football Hall of Fame, Blaik coached three Heisman Trophy winners and numerous All-Americans.

Opposite below is one of West Point's classic sports photographs. Coach Red Blaik is flanked by Heisman Trophy winners Doc Blanchard (35) and Glenn Davis (41).

With the admission of women to West Point, beginning in 1976, the "Rabble Rousers" became co-ed. The photo below was taken in 1977 at Michie Stadium. Note the new artificial turf and A-Man in the center of the picture. This is obviously an early September game as the Corps is donned in white over gray in the background.

At right, a member of the Cadet Parachute Team lands in Michie Stadium on game day in 1999.

This baseball game at Doubleday Field is obviously an important one. The "Hellcats" are present in support of a cadet "march-on." Cullum Hall appears behind the left field fence in the background.

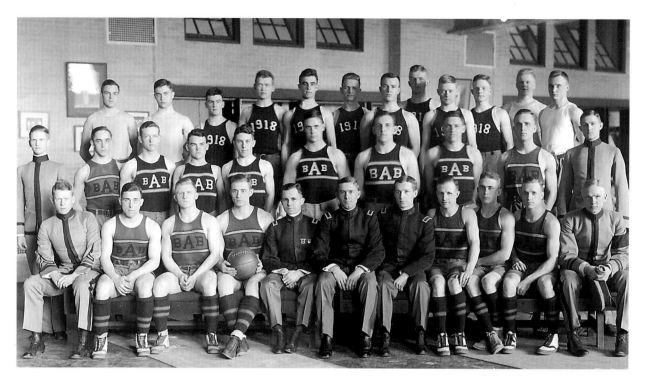

Army's 1915 basketball team displays its stylish uniforms while posing for a team picture in the old gymnasium. The "BAB" on the front of the shirts stand for "Army basketball", and reflects a design that was used on the uniforms of other Army sports teams during the era.

The photo below of the 1966-1967 basketball team was taken in Gillis Fieldhouse, previously the home of Army basketball. Included within the picture are two of Army's most famous basketball celebrities. Cadet Mike Krzyzewski is in the front row (second from right) and Coach Bob Knight is in the back row (second from left).

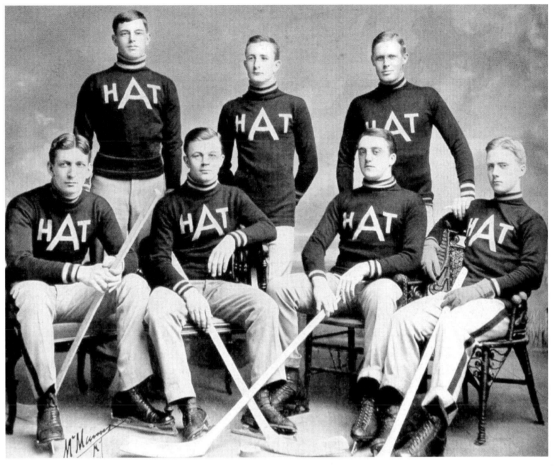

The Army hockey team of 1907 poses for a team picture.

Smith Rink (right) served as the home of Army hockey until the Holleder Center was completed. This photo was taken in the early 1930s. The rink was situated just below Lusk Reservoir on the site of the current Association of Graduates Building.

The Holleder Center (bottom right) is the home of both the Army hockey and basketball teams. The complex was named in honor of Major Donald W. Holleder, class of 1956, who was killed in Vietnam in 1967. The 16-million-dollar facility opened on 1 October 1985. The pucksters play in the 2,746-seat Tate Rink, named in honor of Joseph S. Tate (class of 1941) and his brother, Frederic H.S. Tate (class of 1942), both of whom were pilots who were shot down during World War II. Christl Arena boasts a capacity of 5,043 and provides the home court for the hoopsters. The facility has also hosted a number of other special athletic events such as intercollegiate wrestling, basketball and gymnastics championships, and international volleyball competition.

Physical fitness continues to be an integral part of the cadet academic curriculum. Aside from the intense physical training that is part of the summer military training, cadets are required to take a physical fitness course each semester during the regular academic year. Gymnastics continues to be a required course, normally taken during the plebe year. In this photo, cadets are being instructed on basic tumbling. The current physical fitness uniform is comprised of gym shorts, t-shirt, socks, and tennis shoes and is unquestionably more functional than these uniforms at the turn of the century.

This 1905 picture of cadet wrestling class was taken at the old gymnasium. As in the case of the previous photo of gymnastics and the boxing class below, the physical fitness attire of the day was relatively unimportant. Perhaps the mindset was based on the understanding that soldiers don't change into gym clothes when they are required to employ their physical fitness skills on the battlefield.

In 1905, boxing class was conducted in the appropriate uniform of the day. Boxing remains an integral part of the cadet physical development program. Cadets take boxing during their plebe year. Each of the cadet companies also has a boxing team that competes as part of the winter intramural sports program. Additionally, a Brigade Open is held each year and continues to attract the best boxers from within the Corps.

Arvin Gymnasium
1910

Pictured here in 1915, the gymnasium was renamed in honor of Captain Carl Robert Arvin, Class of 1965, who was killed in Vietnam. Cadet Arvin had excelled in all three dimensions of the West Point program. He was a Rhodes Scholarship finalist (academic), First Captain (military), and captain of the wrestling team (physical).

Shea Stadium

The facility was dedicated in 1958 to Richard Shea, Class of 1952, who gave his life just after graduation on Pork Chop Hill during the Korean War. Shea, who had excelled at track while at the Academy, was posthumously awarded the Medal of Honor. Shea Stadium was recently renovated thanks to alumni donations.

Women's sports are a relatively new, but exciting, component of sports at West Point. Here, pitcher Sarah Hatton (class of 2000) delivers a pitch during Army's first-ever NCAA playoff appearance in Seattle, Washington. The 2000 Army softball team won the Patriot League Championship.

... and a butt ...

Rowing, 1868

Intercollegiate fencing champs, 1904

1915

circa 1920

CHAPTER FIVE

On to the Fray

Military Training

During the summer months all cadets experience intensive military training, although each of the four classes has a different focus. After R-Day, new cadets are housed in the barracks for the majority of "Beast Barracks." Yearlings proceed to Camp Buckner for field training. Cows may travel throughout the world as part of Cadet Troop Leader Training (CTLT) and usually attend a military school (Airborne, Air Assault, Northern Warfare, etc.). Firsties are primarily responsible for training the new cadets and yearlings, and so they assume chain-of-command positions or function as a member of a training committee in Beast or at Buckner. USMA's summer training program is rigorous, "hands-on," and up to date with current doctrine and technology out in the field.

When it comes to physical fitness training (better known as PT), some things have changed (like the stylish uniforms), but other aspects of the training (like the formations and exercises) have endured over the years. Here, new cadets are in the process of organizing into the "extended rectangular formation" in preparation for morning PT on the Plain in the summer of 1920.

Even today, cadets conduct training on how to build a pontoon bridge. Since the photo above, however, the training site has changed from the Hudson River to Lake Stillwell, located northwest of the garrison area near Camp Buckner. In this photograph, the training is occurring in the vicinity of north dock. Constitution Island is visible in the background, as is one of the old Hudson River ferries.

This 1920s photograph reveals cadets in formation during summer camp. The location is adjacent to the Plain near present-day Trophy Point.

While conducting summer training on the Plain might seem impractical today, cadets in the past could receive a lot of instruction very close to the academic area. Here, for example, cadets learn how to operate a coastal artillery gun overlooking the Hudson in 1903.

Above, cadets conduct rifle marksmanship training in the vicinity of North Dock. The Hudson River is in the foreground. Crow's Nest and Storm King mountain are in the background. Target Hill field, at the base of Crow's Nest and to the left, served as the impact area (visible are two white targets at the base of the hill). Presently, Target Hill field hosts intramural athletic competition, but the name originates from the earlier land use as depicted. The original hill was plowed under in the 1940s to widen the area available for sports fields.

The photo above shows yearlings conducting personal hygiene at Camp Buckner during the summer of 1967. Lake Popolopen provides an adequate source of water for the morning shave. White T-shirts of the 60s were replaced with olive drab T-shirts in the 70s and brown T-shirts in the late 80s. Similarly, field uniforms have transitioned from fatigues (as shown) to battle dress uniforms (BDUs).

At right, yearlings receive instruction on land navigation training during their stay at Camp Buckner. This particular training site is located at Lake Frederick. The site remains in use today, overlooking Central Valley in the background.

At the top, the bicentennial class of 2002 marches out onto the Plain late in the afternoon on R-Day as part of the Oath Review. Above, members of the class of 2002 recite the oath prior to marching off for weeks of Cadet Basic Training.

Nearly eight weeks later, "new cadets" of 2002   don their white hats for the first time.
become "cadets" during the Acceptance Day Parade, and

At left and below, members of the class of 2002 conduct hand to hand combat training (now referred to as "close quarters combat" training) in the sawdust pit at Camp Buckner.

At right, yearlings participate in field artillery training at Camp Buckner. Cadets are wearing BDUs and KEVLAR® helmets (previously known as "steel pots").

At Camp Buckner, numerous training exercises and events are intended to foster cooperation and teamwork. In the photo below, a squad of yearlings negotiate the leadership reaction course. Everyone needs to get over the fence without touching the fence itself. This requires teamwork and innovative thinking.

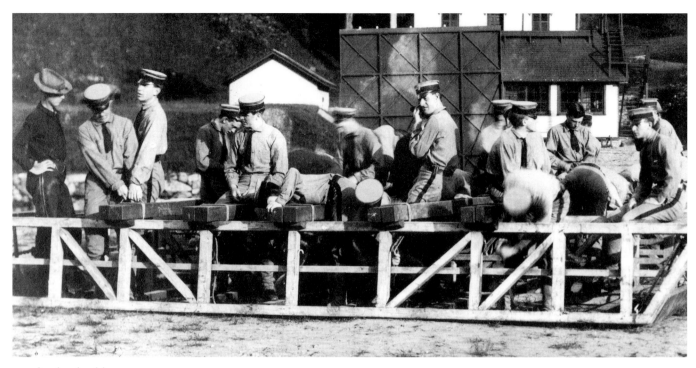

bridge building

... and a butt ...

cavalry practice

ordnance and gunnery training, also known by cadets as...

Ignorance and Gunnery

CHAPTER SIX

Old Soldiers Never Die

Monuments

Monuments serve as icons at West Point. For the most part, they symbolize what every cadet aspires to become. They also serve to showcase for visitors the most accomplished, if not famous, among the Academy's graduates. Whereas the Naval and Air Force Academies boast several monuments that pay tribute to technology, at West Point we pay homage to people. As the Department of History boasts, "Much of the history we teach was made by those we taught."

Sylvanus Thayer
Class of 1808
Instructor, 1809-1811
Superintendent, 1817-1833

Regarded as the "Father of the Military Academy," Colonel Thayer, as a young superintendent, is credited with improving the professionalism of the Corps of Cadets (and thus the Army) and remolding the curriculum to ensure the highest quality of graduates.

COLONEL THAYER,
FATHER
OF THE
MILITARY ACADEMY

George Armstrong Custer
Class of 1861

Despite graduating at the bottom of his class (after someone changed his demerit book) and a post-Civil War court-martial, Custer was remembered by West Pointers for his bravery during the Civil War at Bull Run, Gettysburg and elsewhere, and for his campaigns against Indians in the west. Although first buried on the battlefield at Little Big Horn after his defeat in 1876, his body was moved to the cemetery at West Point in 1877. The statue at lower left was erected in 1879, but was despised by Custer's wife Libby. She thought it made her husband look like a "border ruffian" and accused the sculptor of making Custer look bloodthirsty. The figure was removed at her request in 1884 and replaced with the obelisk shown below. Notice that the pedestals are the same.

Douglas MacArthur
Class of 1903
Superintendent, 1919-1922

Although best known for his service to the nation during World War II, the Japanese Occupation, and the Korean War, MacArthur made lasting contributions during his tenure as superintendent. He supported a liberalization of the curriculum to include more humanities and social science courses. He repeatedly clashed with the Academic Board when they did not accept his world view, and his tenure at West Point was an unhappy time for much of the faculty. Nonetheless, many of his reforms survived his departure and live to the present.

Duty, Honor, Country. Those three hallowed words reverently dictate what you ought to be, what you can be, what you will be. They are your rallying points, to build courage when courage seems to fail, to regain faith when there seems to be little cause for faith, to create hope when hope becomes forlorn.

- 12 May 1962

George S. Patton
Class of 1909

Although not remembered as an outstanding student, George Patton proved himself an excellent officer, serving in both World War I and II. He was also an accomplished athlete, finishing 5th in the modern pentathlon at the 1912 Olympics. The Patton Monument, dedicated in 1950, has four of the General's silver stars melted into the figure. Four embroidered stars, a 3rd Army shoulder patch, and a buffalo nickel designed by the sculptor can be found between the statue and the pedestal. The picture at bottom right, taken in the 1960s, shows the tennis courts that used to be behind the monument.

"End of last lesson in engineering.
Last lesson as cadet. Thank God."
　　　　　　　　　- 1909

Dwight D. Eisenhower
Class of 1915

Below, a retired President Eisenhower breaks ground for the Washington Hall expansion in 1965. To the right, General Eisenhower, in the form of a monument erected in 1983, surveys fire damage on nearby Crow's Nest.

Cadet Monument
1818

This monument, pictured at left in an 1852 image from *Gleason's*, was built in 1818 in memory of a cadet, Vincent Lowe, who was killed by a premature cannon discharge in January of 1817. The base also contains the names of other cadets and faculty who died at West Point.

Dade Monument
1845

Erected in memory of Brevet Major Francis Dade, who, along with 109 of his men, was killed by Seminole Indians in Florida during an operation in 1835. The massacre marked the beginning of the Second Seminole War. The image at right is from *Gleason's Pictorial Drawing-Room Companion*, a 19th-century magazine.

Battle Monument and Sedgwick Monument

Battle Monument dominates the Trophy Point area and commands an excellent view of the Hudson Highlands. Topped by a statue of Fame, the impressive monument was dedicated in 1897 to members of the Regular Army killed during the Civil War. Many Regular Army veterans felt that their contributions had not been properly recognized because of the large number of volunteer militias that fought for the North. The column is recognized as the largest piece of turned granite in the hemisphere. At the base, the names of over 2,000 men are inscribed.

Getting the column in place was quite a challenge. To move the massive piece, railroad tracks were laid up the road from South Dock and across the Plain!

Across the road stands a monument to General John Sedgwick, Class of 1837. Sedgwick was a hero of the Mexican War, and later played a critical role during the Civil War at battles such as Chancellorsville, the Battle of the Wilderness, and Gettysburg. He was killed at the Battle of Spottsylvania in 1864. The statue is reported to be made of cannons captured by the men of his 6th Corps. Legend has it that any cadet in full dress, under arms who spins Sedgewick's spurs the night before a term-end examination, will pass the exam.

The image here shows the dedication of the statue in October of 1868 as depicted in *Harper's Weekly*. It was clearly not a beautiful autumn day.

Ecole Polytechnique
Monument

Presented in 1919 by cadets at the Ecole Polytechnique, this monument, a replica of one on the French campus, commemorates French cadets who defended their country in 1814. The monument is well known for numerous design errors, such as a curved sword but a straight scabbard, and cannonballs too big for the bore of the cannon. Pictured here in 1964 in its original place on the Plain, the statue now resides near the old 1st Division in Central Area.

American Soldiers
Statue

Designed by the sculptor of the Iwo Jima memorial, this monument was dedicated in 1980 by the USMA classes of 1935 and 1936 to honor American soldiers who gave their lives for their country.

PRESENTED TO THE CORPS OF CADE

THE LIVES AND DESTINIES OF VALIANT

ARE ENTRUSTED TO YOUR CARE AND L

CLASS OF 1935   CLA

FELIX de WELDON SCULPTOR 1980

Washington Monument

This monument to our founding father was first unveiled in 1916. For the next 55 years it sat on the northern side of the Plain at the junction of Thayer and Washington roads (left), just east of the Battle Monument. It was moved in 1971 to its current position in front of aptly-named Washington Hall (below).

Kosciusko Monument
1828, 1913

Arriving in America while fleeing the wrath of a vengeful father with whose daughter he had tried to elope, Tadeusz Kosciusko became an indispensible ally of the colonists during the American Revolution. He served first in upstate New York at Fort Ticonderoga and helped the Americans defeat the British at Saratoga. He then came to West Point, spending two years improving the fortifications at Fort Clinton and the surrounding area. He was appointed chief of the engineering corps in 1780. Kosciusko then served in the Carolinas, saving American troops numerous times before orchestrating a successful blockade of Charleston. After the war he was given U.S. citizenship and the rank of brigadier general.

After the Revolution, Kosciusko returned to Poland and led his countrymen for years against Russian and Prussian invaders. He eventually returned to the United States in 1797 and became a close friend of Thomas Jefferson. He eventually retired to France to fight for Polish independence in exile before his death in 1817. An amazing soldier and engineer, he is also remembered for having repeatedly freed serfs in his service.

Kosciusko was so popular with USMA cadets that the Corps of Cadets built a monument to him in 1828. The statue on top of the pedestal, however, was donated in 1913 by the Polish Clergy and Laity of the United States. Kosciusko's personal garden retreat, carved into the slope below Cullum Hall, also remains to this day.

... and a butt ...

CHAPTER SEVEN

Hallowed Ground

Graduates and Guests

Since its founding in 1802, West Point has always managed to attract famous people in either an official or visiting capacity. Indeed, many of its own graduates have become world-renowned. To use an old cliché, success often breeds success. People seem to cherish their association with an institution that aspires to the noble values of duty, honor, and country. The ideals of West Point are embraced by many other successful institutions, and USMA has long been recognized as an example of what "right looks like" as developing countries of the world model their own military academies after West Point.

It is said that after the White House, no home in America has hosted as many important guests as Quarters 100.

Robert E. Lee
Class of 1829
Superintendent,
1852-1855

Lee followed a successful cadet career at West Point with distinguished service in the Corps of Engineers and during the war with Mexico. Captain Lee returned to West Point as superintendent in 1852. Well-liked by cadets for his gentle demeanor, Lee hated disciplining cadets and preferred to give them second chances when possible. He entertained frequently.

In 1855 Lee accepted a cavalry position because it offered a promotion. Current laws required the Supe to be an engineer officer, so Lee had to be replaced. For all northern West Pointers from that period who fought in the Civil War, how strange it must have been to face their well-liked superintendent across the battlefield. A portrait of Lee in Army blue hangs in Quarters 100, a silent reminder of the difficult decisions many West Pointers were required to make as the nation fell apart.

Abner Doubleday
Class of 1842

What did Abner Doubleday do? He fought in the Mexican War during the 1840s, the Seminole War in 1857, and was at Fort Sumter when the Civil War began. In fact, Doubleday is credited with having aimed the first Union shot of that conflict when the Confederate bombardment began. Later he would serve at Sharpsburg, South Mountain, Fredericksburg, Chancellorsville, and Gettysburg, where he helped repel Pickett's Charge. After the war he served for another eight years before retiring in 1873. He died just shy of 20 years later.

What did Abner Doubleday not do? That's right, he did not invent baseball. Although a commission sanctioned by the major leagues determined in 1907 that Doubleday had invented the game in 1839 in Cooperstown, New York, the decision is considered by nearly all historians to be flawed. The head of the commission, Albert Mills, was a former colleague and friend of Doubleday. Some think that the commission was trying to establish the game as "American" and did not want to acknowledge the game's British origins. What evidence is there to prove that Doubleday did not invent the game? First, in 1839 Doubleday was a cadet and was not in Cooperstown. More convincingly, there are written descriptions and even drawings of the game that go back to the early 18th century, nearly 100 years before Doubleday supposedly invented the great American pastime.

Ulysses S. Grant
Class of 1843

Affectionately known to his classmates as Sam, Grant was born Hiram Ulysses Grant in 1822. Interested in West Point not for a military career but as an educational opportunity, Grant enrolled as Ulysses H. Grant, possibly to avoid the initials "H.U.G." on his gear. A clerical error made him Ulysses S. Grant, and cadets gave him a nickname of "Sam," as in "Uncle Sam" Grant. While at the Academy, he took interest in drawing and horsemanship. Mathematics was also a strong subject for the son of Ohio. After graduation Grant served with distinction during the war with Mexico. Less than exciting postings after the war, separation from his family, and possibly alcohol use eventually led to his resignation from the Army in 1854. He attempted farming in Missouri for a few years before joining a family-run leather business in Illinois.

Pulled back into service by the Civil War, Grant was made a general. He won the first major victory for the Union Army by demanding the unconditional surrender of troops at Fort Donelson in Tennessee during the winter of 1862. He rose to the command of all Union troops in 1864 and led the North to victory.

Grant's popularity led him to the White House in the elections of 1868. His presidency was marked by scandal, but Grant fought hard for the civil rights of ex-slaves and sought to rebuild the South by granting amnesty for Confederate soldiers and by supporting Reconstruction laws. An international celebrity after his time in office, Grant traveled extensively before his death in 1885.

General Grant reviewing the Corps of Cadets in 1865.

John J. Pershing
Class of 1886

A First Captain as a cadet, Pershing went on to fight during the Spanish-American War in the Philippines. Later, as a general, Pershing was the leader of all U.S. forces in World World I. In 1959 the West Academic Building was renamed Pershing Barracks in his honor. As shown below, Eisenhower Hall was almost named Pershing Hall. At the bottom, Pershing (left) revisits West Point during the tenure of Superintendent Douglas MacArthur (right).

Omar N. Bradley
Class of 1915
Instructor of Mathematics, 1919-1923

His most prominent characteristic is "getting there", and if he keeps up the clip he's started, some of us will someday be bragging to our grandchildren that "sure, General Bradley was a classmate of mine."
-*The Howitzer*, 1915

As the *Howitzer* quote reveals, Omar Bradley's classmates sensed greatness in his presence. After leaving the Academy, Bradley commanded the 82nd and 28th Infantry Divisions. During World War II he led the II Corps in North Africa and Sicily. In 1944, as commander of the 1st Army, he invaded Normandy and liberated Paris. His successes led to his being named the commander of the U.S. 12th Army Group, which fought throughout central Europe. After the war, he served as head of veteran's affairs and as Chief of Staff of the Army before becoming the first Chairman of the Joint Chiefs of Staff. His classmates were right.

OMAR NELSON BRADLEY
MOBERLY, MISSOURI

Appointed from Second District, Missouri

"Brad"

Sergeant, First Sergeant, Lieutenant; Sharpshooter; Football Squad (2, 1); "A" in Football; Baseball Squad (4, 3, 2, 1); "A" in Baseball; Indoor Meet (3, 2); V.C.

"True merit is like a river, the deeper it is, the less noise it makes"—Anon

The Roosevelts

FDR at graduation, 1939

Eleanor visits, 1951

John F. Kennedy
Graduation, June 1962

Theodore Roosevelt
Calvin P. Titus
11 June 1902

While serving as a bugler with E Company, 14th U.S. Infantry in Beijing in 1900 during the Boxer Rebellion, Trumpeter Calvin P. Titus responded to a request for a volunteer to scale the walls of the city with, "I'll try, sir." Titus was successful and soon received an appointment to West Point. During centennial activities in June of 1902, plebe Titus was surprised by President Roosevelt, who can be seen here pinning on the Medal of Honor Titus earned for his courage.

Gerald Ford
Graduation, 1975

Ronald Reagan
1987

Bob Hope
Thayer Award recipient, 1968

... and a butt ...

Red Skelton, 1978

Bob Hope, 1970

Marie Osmond, 1986

Cadet Norman Schwartzkopf, Class of 1956

General Albert L. Mills
Superintendent, 1898-1906,
Medal of Honor Winner

The Association of Graduates, 1911

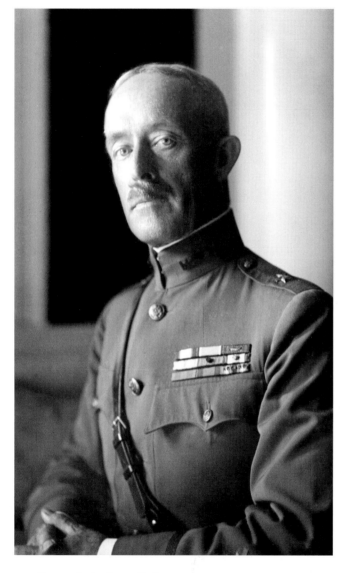

General Fred W. Sladen
Class of 1890
Commandant of Cadets, 1911-1914
Superintendent, 1922-1926

Cadet George W. Goethals
Class of 1880
Builder of the Panama Canal

CHAPTER EIGHT

Gray Walls

Architecture

The imposing architectural landscape of West Point does more than simply serve as a backdrop for the impressive history of the Academy. The building styles here represent a snapshot of American history, reflecting popular trends and fashions. It also sheds light on an Academy trying to establish itself by finding an architectural theme to represent the moral-ethical development it seeks to foster in cadets.

Quarters 100
1820

Almost the oldest in-use building on post (some date the Commandant's House to 1819), the Superintendent's House is one of the most famous homes in America. It possesses typical features of the Federal period (1780-1820), such as the narrow chimneys on the ends of the house, the symmetrical windows with double-hung sashes and six panes, and the teeth-like dentils on the cornice. The porch and guest quarters at the back were added later. Built during the tenure of Sylvanus Thayer, the building served as post headquarters for several years. Claims that the building is haunted have persisted for years.

Old Cadet Chapel
1836, moved 1911

Built only 15 years after Quarters 100, the Old Chapel represents a shift in American architecture to a Classic style drawing on both Greek and Roman features. The front pediment and Doric columns are Grecian, while the arches over the doors and windows speak to Roman styles. The chapel originally sat next to the library on the site of what is now Bartlett Hall, but was moved to the West Point Cemetery in 1911 with the completion of a new chapel. The building is well known for the mural over the altar, painted by USMA faculty member Robert Weir, who also painted the *Landing of the Pilgrims* in the U.S. Capitol Building, and for the infamous plaque for Benedict Arnold that has been defaced to remind of Arnold's treason.

Second Academy Building
1838-1895

After the first Academy was destroyed by fire in 1838, work began on this large building. It was a simple building without a great deal of architectural flourish. The addition of the columns on the front and the arches above some windows suggests an attempt was made to complement the Cadet Chapel which stood just out of the picture to the left.

Old Library
1841-1961

Library, West Point, N.Y.

Constructed just five years after the Old Cadet Chapel and three years after the Second Academy, the Old Library represented yet another change in architectural style. This time, a Tudor style was emphasized. The battlements at the ends of the building and the castellated decoration along the top of the building are characteristically Tudor. In addition to housing books, the Old Library served as post headquarters, and included classrooms and a large observatory. The astronomy equipment was housed in three separate towers, the largest one (visible in the top picture) contained a domed roof mounted on 24 cannonballs as bearings. The observatory was later moved near Lusk Reservoir.

Grant Hall (Old Cadet Mess)
1852-1929

Constructed to replace the old mess hall that stood on the Plain (the last building to do so), the new facility continued the trend of castle-like construction, boasting towers and battlements. It was, of course, not known as Grant Hall when first built. It was located on Thayer Road on the same site as the current Grant Hall and Grant Barracks (formerly South Barracks).

Central Barracks & Support Buildings
North Wing, 1851
West Wing (pictured) 1882

The various wings of Central Barracks continued the Tudor style. The castellated towers and battlements are still present, and the addition of sallyports, now such an important part of the West Point landscape, were also Tudor in design. The support building closest to the barracks served as the Commandant's office. Notice the signs of heavy foot traffic in and out. The middle building housed the steam boilers and possibly the showers. Again the foot traffic suggests heavy cadet use. The closest building was a power utility building as evidenced by the smokestack.

Old Administration Building
1870-1910

The late 1800s witnessed a variety of architectural styles that created a diverse West Point landscape that often clashed. One example is the Old Administration Building that served as post headquarters. Built in 1870 on what would now be the southern end of Bartlett Hall, this building combined the Second Empire era of American architecture (1855-1885) with Gothic Revival (1840-1880) elements. The mansard roof is classically French Second Empire, but the tower and windows seem to reflect Gothic stylings.

This photograph shows the location of the Administration Building along Thayer Road.

Old Gymnasium
1885-1924

This impressive but somewhat out-of-place gymnasium stood at the southwest corner of the Plain on the current site of Washington Hall. It was demolished in 1924 to make way for Washington Hall.

West Academic Building
(Pershing Barracks)
1895

Built in 1895, the West Academic Building, seen at left from the back, and below with a tower that was never added, incorporated elements from surrounding buildings. The shape of the building created the natural quadrangle that is now Central Area. The sallyports also connected it with the neighboring barracks. The battlements on the top created continuity with the barracks and with the library across Thayer Road. The small towers on each side of the sallyports were similar to those found on Grant Hall next door. Later renamed Pershing Barracks, the West Academic Building stands as one of the first attempts to create new buildings that harmonized with older structures.

Cullum Hall
1896

George Cullum was a Class of 1833 graduate, Civil War general, and USMA superintendent (1864-1866) who felt that West Point needed a building to house trophies and to honor distinguished officers and graduates of the Academy. A wealthy author, Cullum donated $200,000 for the construction. With its return to classical motifs, many today think that the building looks out of place, but at the time of its construction it was fairly close to the old cadet chapel which also had a classical design. Notice the old location of the Dade Monument in front of the building. The monument now resides in the West Point Cemetery.

Catholic Chapel
1900

Jewish Chapel
1984

Cadet Chapel
1910

As the 20th century opened, the Academy welcomed a great deal of internal debate about what architectural style should dominate the West Point landscape. Many older buildings were in need of replacement, so a jury was convened to decide whether new buildings should follow classical lines, like Cullum Hall and the Old Cadet Chapel, Tudor stylings, like the barracks, or the eclectic design of the West Academic Building. The winning style was none of these. Gothic architecture was decided upon with the stipulation that new buildings should try to mesh with existing structures.

The New Cadet Chapel stands as a beautiful example of the new Gothic era. Pointed arches, stone carving, and stained glass make it one of the finest Gothic churches in America. Its organ, begun in 1911, is the largest church organ in the world.

Headquarters Building
(Taylor Hall)
1909

Although not strongly evident, the new headquarters building also is considered a Gothic building, with pointed arches and intricate stone work scattered throughout, much of it out of the public eye. At 160 feet tall, it is reported to be the tallest solid masonry structure on the planet.

Washington Hall
1928, addition 1965

Washington Hall continued the Gothic building trend at West Point and added a much needed larger mess hall. The pointed arch on the front of the original building is a sure giveaway, as is the detailed stone in the front windows. In this picture the building is so new that the ornamental crest has not yet been added to the front. When the building was expanded in 1965, the original facade was kept and can now be seen within the interior of the building.

West Point Hotel
1829-1932

Hotel Thayer
1926

... and a butt ...

Benny Haven's

South Train Station, 1926

South Gate, 1902

Riding Hall

Building South Road, 1903

CHAPTER NINE

Sons of Slum and Gravy

Perceptions of West Point

There are many West Points. There is West Point the symbol of national pride; West Point the tourist destination; West Point the sports venue; West Point the school; and even West Point the prison. This chapter focuses (lightly) on how West Point has been used as an advertising symbol and how cadets view the Academy. The views are not always consistent.

While beating Navy is never easy, more cadets have struggled to "Beat the Dean," housed in the mighty fortress that is Taylor Hall

A not-so-flattering *Howitzer* entry from early in the 20th Century. In "Kaydet" lingo, to skin was to write someone up. In other words, to turn in your fellow cadets.

"Cadets who have occasion to record delinquencies shall do so in person." Par. 21 h, Blue Book.

Nervy Nat has found that regulation frightfully inconvenient ever since he joined the aggregation of bootlicknoids who help the "Com" to keep the number of Christmas leaves from becoming excessive... Skin, skin, skin, nothing to do but skin—how nice to be a file-closer and sting all the boys in ranks! But say, you ought to hear the wail Nervy sends up when some section marcher gets him for a late. It's funny, isn't it, what a difference it makes whether we are the skinoid or the skinee?"

From a 1926 *Howitzer*, a cadet view of the perfect West Point. Notice the easy R-Day, hanging the buglers (Hell-Cats), free food and entertainment, a dungeon for officers, free time, etc.

Beginning with improved boat access from New York City in the early to mid-1800s, a stop at West Point became a necessary one on any visit to the region. Foreign tourists would come to New York from Europe, cruise up the Hudson, travel to Niagara Falls, and then return. The perfect American holiday. And don't forget to send a postcard ...

This 19th-century magazine engraving shows how West Point was romanticized in the popular media. This depiction of Kosciuszko's Garden makes the small retreat look like the Garden of Eden, complete with Adam and Eve.

And why not take West Point home with you ...

GLOVES SINCE 1854

REGULATION AT WEST POINT FOR MANY YEARS

Daniel Hays Gloves

Decades before women were admitted to the   early *Howitzer* drawing suggests.
Academy, some cadets thought it was a good idea, as this

130

In 1915, cadets thought that West Point would be a good subject for the growing movie industry ...

... and a butt ...

A fake ad from an old *Howitzer*. Some perceptions never change ...

THE CADET MESS

AN UNRIVALLED EATING AND CHOP HOUSE WITHIN EASY REACH OF THE HOSPITAL

Our own specially prepared dishes have defied the qualitative analysis of food specialists for years. An excellent field of research for Curiosity Dealers, Mineralogists, Bacteriologists and Epicureans.

RULES OF THE HOUSE

1. No live dogs allowed in the building
2. Don't swear at the waiter, the O. D. may hear you
3. Don't kick, we have the riding hall reserved for that purpose
4. Don't drop any dishes or money on the floor
5. Don't bring an appetite, or else we will be compelled to relieve you of it
6. Do not throw potatoes at the pictures on the wall

SPECIAL DELICACIES

Slum Gudgeon—our " chef do over" permutations and combinations infinite　　Blue Mud

Franklinite Meat Balls　　　　Fish Every Friday—morning, noon and night　　　　Boiled Milk

Oleomargarine　　　Sammy　　　Stuffed Leather Beefsteak　　　Side dishes to order

A circa 1900 *Harper's Weekly* exposé on hazing featured this popular plebe activity, known as "swimming to Newburgh."

This fake product from 1968 shows that cadets are not always happy with their lives at the Academy.

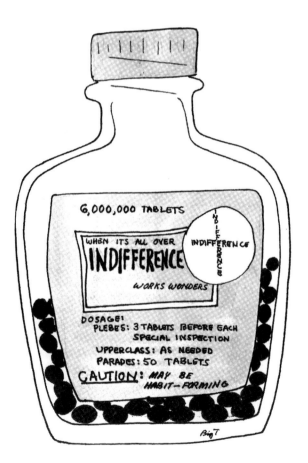

Taps

Our intent within the context of this historical-geographical portfolio has been to shed light on the enduring "spirit" of West Point. It is the spirit that enables the place not only to endure but to transcend the ages. Perhaps we should have entitled our book *The First 200 Years*, because the vitality of the institution and the high expectations of the American society, if not the global community, ensure the sanctity of the place for the foreseeable future.

Although we entitle our conclusion as "taps" (a traditional military bugle call signaling "lights out" at the end of the day), rest assured that when the sun comes up tomorrow and the bugler sounds "reveille," West Point will continue to epitomize for many people around the world the values of duty, honor, and country.

... The Long Gray Line ...
Graduation Parade, 2000

Credits

Most of the images in this book are from the United States Military Academy Archives (including the Special Collections Division of the USMA Library), with the following exceptions:

Jon Malinowski: 4, 26, 56 (top), 59 (bottom), 63, 80 (right), 82 (right), 84, 87, 88 (bottom), 89 (right), 90 (top left), 106, 134, 135

Collection of the authors: 89

Robert A. Getz: 9, 29, 41, 51, 67, 77, 91, 105, 112 (middle), 116 (bottom), 123, 138

Department of Geography and Engineering, USMA: 13, 15, 16, 17, 18, 23, 24, 25, 27 (bottom), 28, 44, 45, 46, 47, 48, 49, 50, 66, 71 (bottom), 78, 79 (right), 82 (left), 86, 93 (bottom), 95 (middle), 98 (top right), 103 (top right & bottom), 104, 118

Association of Graduates, USMA: 109 (bottom), 120 (left), 126 (bottom)

Sports Information Office, USMA: 64

Directorate of Information Management (DOIM), USMA: front & back covers, 31 (right), 72, 73, 74, 75

Andy Lohman & Jon Malinowski: 141

Bibliography

Boynton, Edward C. (1867). *Guide to West Point and the U.S. Military Academy*. New York: D. Van Nostrand.

Bugle Notes (various years). West Point: United States Military Academy.

Crackel, Theodore (1991). *The Illustrated History of West Point*. New York: H.N. Abrams.

Gray, David W. (1951). "The Architectural Development of West Point." Unpublished manuscript, Department of Military Topography and Graphics, United States Military Academy.

The Howitzer (various years). West Point, NY: United States Military Academy.

Moses, Edward M. (1995). *West Point: The Making of Leaders, An Historical Sketchbook*. Robert A. Getz, Illustrator. West Point, NY: Edward M. Moses and Robert A. Getz.

Rifkind, Carole (1980). *A Field Guide to American Architecture*. New York: Plume.

Robert A. Getz

Robert A. Getz, a graphic designer from the Hudson Valley in New York, began his formal fine arts instruction at Dean Junior College in Massachusetts. While at Dean, he was elected to *Who's Who Among Students in Junior Colleges* in recognition of his outstanding accomplishments. At graduation, Mr. Getz received the Trustee Award for Excellence in Art. He then enrolled in New York State University College at Buffalo where he graduated with a Bachelor of Science Degree in Design. His artistic and design skills have led him into several career fields, including advertising, architectural design, and publishing. He is currently a staff member of the Department of Geography and Environmental Engineering at the United States Military Academy at West Point. Assignments at West Point have included computer graphics, animation, multi-media, and illustrations. He also provides illustrations for the Association of Graduates alumni magazine *Assembly*. Mr. Getz has lectured on visualization, color, and design as it relates to computer technology, and he has exhibited his work throughout New England and New York. He has worked in a wide variety of media, including painting, sculpture and pen & ink. He and his wife, Johnnie Lou, currently live in Newburgh, New York.

Mr. Getz has illustrated two books about the United States Military Academy. The pen & ink illustrations in this book, along with over 150 illustrations relating to West Point and its leaders, are available and make great graduation, retirement, and promotion gifts. Prints and print sets can be ordered by contacting Robert A. Getz, 153 Hickory Hill Rd., Newburgh, New York 12550. bgetz@hotmail.com

Thanks

The authors would like to thank the United States Military Academy Association of Graduates for their enthusiasm, Ms. Suzanne Christoff and the staff of the USMA Archives for their patience, Deborah Allen and the staff at Black Dome Press, proofreader Matina H. Billias, our families for their loving support, and the Corps of Cadets for their energy and dedication.

We would also like to thank the following companies for allowing us to use certain images:

Exxon Mobil Corporation: page 122 (Socony)
Faribault Foods: page 122 (Empson's Peas)
Gates-Mills, Inc.: page 124 (Daniel Hays Gloves)

About the Authors

Jon C. Malinowski, Ph.D. is an Associate Professor of Geography at the United States Military Academy. A 1991 graduate of Georgetown University and a 1995 graduate of the University of North Carolina at Chapel Hill, Dr. Malinowski is also the co-author of *The Summer Camp Handbook*. His research interests include human spatial behavior, children's place preferences, and Asia.

Eugene J. Palka, Ph.D. is an Academy Professor and Director of the Geography Program at the United States Military Academy. Colonel Palka is a 1978 graduate of West Point and holds a master's degree from Ohio University and a doctorate from the University of North Carolina at Chapel Hill. He is also the author of *Valued Landscapes of the Far North: A Geographic Journey Through Denali National Park*. His research interests include military, cultural, and historical geography.